MARK McGWIRE

MARK
McGWIRE

BOB TEMPLE
THE CHILD'S WORLD®, INC.

ON THE COVER...

Front cover: Mark gets ready to hit another homer during a 1999 game.
Page 2: Mark prepares for batting practice at Pro Player Stadium in Miami on September 3, 1998.

Library of Congress Cataloging-in-Publication Data
Temple, Bob.
Mark McGwire / by Bob Temple.
p. cm.
Includes index.
ISBN 1-56766-830-5 (lib. bdg. : alk. paper)
1. McGwire, Mark, 1963——Juvenile literature.
2. Baseball players—United States—Biography—Juvenile literature.
[1. McGwire, Mark, 1963– 2. Baseball players.]
GV865.M369 T46 2000b
796.357'092—dc21
00-040493

PHOTO CREDITS

© AP/Wide World Photos: 2, 6, 9, 10, 13, 15, 16, 19, 20, 22
© Rob Tringali, Jr./SportsChrome-USA: cover

TABLE OF CONTENTS

A SHORT HIT, BUT A BIG ONE

The most important home run of Mark McGwire's career was also one of the shortest. And it was one of the quickest. On September 8, 1998, Mark needed only one home run to break the **Major League Baseball** record for home runs in a season. Roger Maris set the record of 61 homers in 1961. The record hadn't been challenged in the 37 years since, but Mark had tied it the day before. With almost a month left in the season, he was sure to break it. The only question was when.

Mark didn't waste any time. In the fourth inning, Mark's bat connected with a pitch from Steve Trachsel of the Chicago Cubs. Mark's homers usually travel a long way, but this one shot like a low-flying rocket. It cruised over the left-field fence, giving Mark 62 home runs for the season—a new record. By the end of the season, Mark would have 70 home runs. The record-setting homer was the shortest of them all, traveling only 341 feet.

Mark hits his record-breaking 62nd home run against the Chicago Cubs on September 8, 1998.

BORN TO HIT HOME RUNS

Mark was born on October 1, 1963, in Pomona, California. He was the third of five boys in the McGwire family. All of them grew very tall. Mark grew to be six-foot-five. The boys were also athletic. Mark's brother Dan grew up to play quarterback for the Seattle Seahawks of the National Football League.

Before he was done playing Little League, Mark was already setting home-run records. At age seven, he hit a home run in his first **at-bat** in Little League. The pitcher he was facing that time was 12 years old! When Mark was only 10 years old, he set the Claremont (California) Little League record for home runs with 13.

ALMOST GAVE IT UP

Even though Mark was always a great hitter, he didn't always want to be one. When he was a sophomore in high school, Mark quit the baseball team to play golf. When he returned to baseball, Mark got noticed more as a pitcher than a hitter. In June of 1981, the Montreal Expos chose Mark in the major-league **draft.** The Expos wanted him to be a pitcher. Instead of signing, he accepted a **scholarship** to the University of Southern California.

Mark pitching for the University of Southern California in 1982.

→

1984 IS A BIG YEAR

In his first year of college, Mark gave up pitching and began playing first base all the time. In 1984, he set a record for home runs at the University of Southern California. He hit 32 in just 67 games in that season. Later that year, Mark was again chosen in the draft, this time by the Oakland A's. But he had one more accomplishment before he signed his pro **contract.** In 1984, baseball was played in the Olympics for the first time. Mark played on the United States team. That team won the gold medal.

A PRIZED ROOKIE

Mark finally made it to the major leagues in 1987. He quickly impressed his teammates and opponents with his power. It didn't take him long to start setting records. Mark set the record for home runs by a **rookie,** hitting 49 for the A's. He had a chance to hit his 50th in the last game of the season. He decided to miss the game, however, to be with his wife, Kathy. She was in the hospital to have their first baby. "I will never have another first-born, but I will have another chance to hit 50 [home runs]," Mark said. Right he was.

Mark hits his first major-league grand slam on August 12, 1988.

THE WORLD SERIES

Mark got a chance to play in the **World Series** two years in a row. The first time, in 1988, Mark had only one hit in five games, and the A's lost to the Los Angeles Dodgers. The next year, though, Mark made up for it. He didn't hit a single home run, but he batted .343, and the A's defeated the San Francisco Giants to win the World Series.

TOUGH TIMES ON THE FIELD

In 1990, Mark hit 39 home runs to become the first player to hit at least 30 homers in each of his first four full seasons. But not everything was going well for Mark. His batting average was going down, and some people were criticizing him for trying to hit home runs all the time. They thought he should try to have a better batting average.

So Mark changed his swing. In 1991, he had his worst season. He hit only 22 homers and batted just .201. He needed to make some changes.

"I decided I wouldn't fight it," Mark said. "That is what I am—a home-run hitter." Mark stopped worrying about his batting average, and he hit 42 home runs in 1992. And, even though he wasn't worrying about it, his average soared to .268.

Mark leaps into the air as he celebrates with his Oakland A's teammates after winning the 1989 World Series.

Just when he was getting back to hitting home runs, Mark had more setbacks. From 1993 to 1995, Mark missed a total of 290 games because of injuries. He hurt his heels, his back, and his ribs.

Mark was discouraged, but he didn't give up. He watched lots of baseball games while he was hurt. "I learned a lot just watching," he said. "I learned much more on the mental side. I learned how to stay positive." Once he got healthy, Mark returned to hitting home runs. In 1995, he hit 39 home runs. The next year, he finally reached the 50 mark, hitting 52 homers for the A's.

TRADED AWAY

In 1997, Mark had his best year yet. It was also a difficult year, however. Mark started the year hitting lots of homers for the A's, but there was trouble in Oakland. The team was losing money, and since Mark had a big contract, the A's needed to trade him. On July 31, the A's traded Mark to the St. Louis Cardinals. The fans in St. Louis were thrilled to have him on their team.

"I came to St. Louis, and the people just overwhelmed me," Mark said. "I've never felt anything like that." He hit 24 homers in the final two months of the season, giving him a total of 58 for the year. For the first time, Mark believed he could break Maris's record of 61 home runs in a season.

Mark hits a homer in the eighth inning against the San Franciso Giants on September 9, 1997.

→

MORE THAN JUST BASEBALL

Mark is more than just a great hitter. He is also a good person. Mark believes in helping people, especially children, who are less fortunate than he is. Near the end of the 1997 season, Mark signed a new contract with the Cardinals. But he didn't keep all of the money for himself. Instead, he gave $3 million to the Mark McGwire Foundation for Children. Mark uses that foundation to help children who have been abused.

THE MOST EVER

No one had ever hit 62 home runs in a season in the major leagues. Mark started out the 1998 season hot, hitting a grand slam in the first game of the season. By the middle of June, he already had 31 homers. It was clear that, unless he got hurt, Mark would set a new record. But it wasn't clear if he would be the first one to get there. Another player, Sammy Sosa of the Chicago Cubs, was also chasing Maris's record. The competition between the two sluggers was friendly, however. They both wished each other well.

Cameras and reporters surround Mark in August of 1998 and ask him about the race for the home run record.

Mark wasn't just on his way to hitting the most homers. He was also hitting them farther than anyone else. In May, he hit a ball 545 feet to center field at Busch Stadium in St. Louis. It was the longest home run in the history of the stadium. "It's the best ball I've ever hit," Mark said. "I don't think I can hit a better one than that."

CHASING THE RECORD

On September 1, Mark hit his 56th and 57th homers, setting a new National League record. Maris's total of 61 homers was the only record left to break. On September 8, Mark did it. The ball shot out of the stadium, and Mark started jumping and celebrating. He was so excited, he went right past first base without touching it. He had to go back and step on it. When he got to home plate, his son, Matthew, was there waiting for him.

Mark broke the record against the Cubs, and Sammy Sosa was playing in the game. Sosa ran in from right field to celebrate with Mark. Mark also went into the stands and hugged Roger Maris's children, who came to see him set the record.

Sammy Sosa came all the way in from right field to congratulate Mark on his record-breaking 62nd homer.

→

Mark had been the player to break Maris's record, but he still wasn't sure if he'd end up with the most home runs that season. Sammy Sosa was still close. On September 25, Sammy passed Mark by hitting his 66th homer of the season. Later that day, Mark also hit his 66th homer to tie Sammy. Mark finished the season with five homers in the last three games. He ended up with 70 home runs. Many people had thought no one would ever break Maris's record. Hardly anyone thought a player would ever hit 70 home runs in one season. Mark proved them all wrong.

"I can't believe I did that," Mark said. "It's absolutely amazing."

MORE MILESTONES

In the 1999 season, Mark didn't reach 70 homers again, but he came close. In the first three months of the season, he hit just 23 home runs, and it seemed that another miracle season was out of reach. But in July, Mark hit 16 home runs in just 25 games, and the chase was on again.

On August 5, he reached another milestone, becoming just the 17th player in history to hit 500 home runs in his career. Later in the year, he became one of the first players to reach 60 home runs two years in a row. He finished the season with 65 home runs and now ranks 10th on the all-time list, with 522. If he continues to be healthy, Mark could become only the fourth player to reach 600 home runs!

Mark connected with his 500th career home run against the San Diego Padres at Busch Stadium in St. Louis.

TIMELINE

October 1, 1963	Mark McGwire is born in Pomona, California.
June 1981	Mark is drafted by the Montreal Expos as a pitcher. Instead of signing a pro contract, he accepts a baseball scholarship to the University of Southern California.
1984	Now a first baseman, Mark hits 32 homers in 67 games, tying USC's career home-run record in just one season.
1987	In his first season with the Oakland A's, Mark sets the major-league record for home runs by a rookie, with 49.
October 1989	Mark leads Oakland to the World Series championship.
1993–95	Mark misses 290 games over three seasons with a variety of injuries.
1996	After a heel injury in March, Mark considers retiring. He returns, and later that season he becomes the 13th player in history to hit 50 homers in a season.
July 31, 1997	The A's trade Mark to the St. Louis Cardinals. Eight days later, he hits a home run in his first game in Busch Stadium.
September 28, 1997	Mark finishes the season with 58 home runs.
September 7, 1998	Mark ties Roger Maris's record of 61 homers in a season.
September 8, 1998	Mark hits the record-breaking 62nd homer off Steve Trachsel of the Chicago Cubs.
September 27, 1998	Mark ends the season by hitting two homers in his final game, giving him a record total of 70 for the season.
August 5, 1999	Mark hits the 500th home run of his career, becoming just the 17th player ever to reach that mark.
October, 1999	Mark is one of 30 players named to Major League Baseball's All-Century Team.

Mark tips his cap to the crowd at a ceremony celebrating his 500th career home run on August 5, 1999.

GLOSSARY

at-bat (at–BAT)
Each player's turn to bat in a baseball game is called an at-bat. Mark McGwire hit a home run in his first at-bat in Little League.

contract (KON–trakt)
A contract is the form an athlete signs when he or she agrees to play for a team. Mark McGwire donated $3 million to charity when he signed his new contract with the St. Louis Cardinals.

draft (DRAFT)
When baseball players get picked by teams, it is called a draft. Mark McGwire was first drafted by the Montreal Expos as a pitcher.

Major League Baseball (MAY–jer LEEG BAYS–ball)
The top level of professional baseball is called Major League Baseball. Mark McGwire broke the Major League Baseball record for home runs in a season.

rookie (ROOK–ee)
A player in his first year in Major League Baseball is called a rookie. Mark McGwire hit 49 home runs as a rookie, a new record.

scholarship (SKAH–ler–ship)
A scholarship is money given to a student to help pay for college. Mark McGwire got a scholarship to the University of Southern California.

World Series (WURLD SEER–eez)
The championship of Major League Baseball is called the World Series. Mark McGwire helped the Oakland A's win the World Series in 1989.

INDEX